...and Touches

of Nature

By Dudley (CHRIS) Christian

A

Pause For Poetry ©

Publication

Acknowledgement:

Special thanks to my wife, Marilyn Christian for compiling, organizing and finalizing the books of my collections. Her photographing and editing skills were vital to all of my works.

ISBN: 978-0-9916853-5-6

First Edition December 2012
Revised Edition June 2017

Cover: Belcarra Bay, BC with insets of views from the area © Marilyn Christian

<u>An Opening Word by the Author...</u>

Many people often ask:

"How do you write and do you have to often rewrite your material?"

I have long summed up my answer to the above with the following:

"A Word, the written word, small purveyor of a thought, so like a thought, once thought, cannot be recalled, so too, a word once writ, should need NOT be re-written, for with such licence, we would but change ... the very substance of the thought."

... DNC © 1970

Dudley (Chris) Christian founded and hosted the first and only "PAUSE FOR POETRY" show dedicated solely to the introduction of new and unknown poets and their works. This TV series ran from 1974 to 1985.

Table of Contents

Dear Reader:

Just a light touch along Love's and Life's highways, giving you I hope, a deeper insight into that most elusive of paths we all will walk down one day, or at least we hope we will...

Come take a glance, and a chance, as "I Come To The Sea Alone" (page 30) ; they that go down to the sea in ships even as we go "Down The Trail From Mountain Pass" (page 42). Then, hand in hand, listen to the tide's chorus, as you also "Bind Tightly Thy Love" (page 76) while you glimpse more scenes of high hills, far away valley fields and distant water-spots of Rivers, of Oceans, and of Seas.

Go back, smile and recall those jovial times you played the further games of love. Re-take those "Pledges Of Love" (page 72). Take a wish back into "That Just Loved Look" (page 78) in your "Memories of You" (page 77) before skipping along past, or into "The Virgin's Demands" (page 82) .

Smile, smile or outright laugh, laugh, laugh at yourself as you look back, back to what you thought you'd gladly die for and realize now it truly was (as biblical Solomon said) 'Vanity... just Vanity'.

In Cold or Warm or Calm or Storm

In cold or warm or calm or storm
You hold in awe and wonder
My every thought each time I see
You break or roll or thunder.
You imitator of the skies
Of all that pass of colour
Your soft yet steady tides
Moves on it seems forever.
You paint yourself in every hue
From dawn to dusk each day
Then sparkle in the moonlight too
When the sun has passed away.
You are so soft and gentle wave
As you lap along the shore
That one would seldom comprehend
What you have done before.
In search of life or venture bold
You traverse 'round the earth
Seeking it seems but once to hold
The one who gave you birth.
Oh little wave so whitely crested
By bubbling misty spray
Roll on and on and ever on
But from my heart please never stray.

We Met By Chance

We met by chance
We never had a chance
A chance to get to know each other
And yet tho short the time
I knew without a doubt
Without a feeling of uncertainty
I knew when you I'd known
When you within my arms I'd held
Love it was ours then forever
For deep within I loved you
And you knew.

I loved you with a passion
Not in a passionate way
But with a passion that endures
A passion that endures the time
A passion that outlives the doubts
A passion to live 'til you are mine
Such a passion as can only once
In life itself be felt by one
And thus it was I knew full well
That soon tho you'd be gone away
That I alone would thinking lay

Upon my lonesome bed at night
Yet there my heart would be content
My soul and body would feel right
For once we met and touched
And love was ours forever
As deep within I loved you
And you knew.

You -- frail-like -- like a bird doth seem
Came to me like a dream
A gossamer dream from heaven
To share my day my evening time as well
And then alas my night and too my bed
You gave not yourself to me that night
Nor did you wait me myself to give
But like one thought one vision
Like one dream to be fulfilled
We came together in contentedness
And we for each other shared
And we for each other cared
Then all was right within our world
For love was ours forever
And deep within I loved you
And you knew...

Of such dreams are life made
Of such moments does love grow
Of such unaccountable reasons we
Will some how or time or place
Within another stranger place
Completely all our trust
We gave each other all we had to give
We gave each other cause to live
To carry on thru dark of life
To fight and win the dreary strife
Which sought our paths to cross
For we together pooled our strength
And reached across life's oceans length
To find what deep lay hidden there
Love that was ours forever
For deep within I loved you
And you knew.

Thus fate may try to mock our love
Pitfalls may place affront us now
To test the strength we knew
Still I will stand beside you proud
And shout at all the leering crowd
What we knew then was love
Then challenge them I, 'come and say
That we should ever rue the day

No matter what of it may come'
For from such unison as we knew
Such love as shared by me and you
Could be but borne a love child too
And this they can't deny.
Then laugh out if fate so demands
We'll raise our love child with our hands
Which held to each other's love commands
When love it was ours forever
Love it was ours forever
For deep within I loved you then
And know you feel it e'er again
Each time your thoughts return

We met by chance
We never had a chance
A chance to get to know each other
And yet tho short the time
I knew your love was mine
I knew our love was ours forever
For deep within I loved you
And deep within you knew

Notice even waves lap the shoreline
in seemingly pleasurable motions

I Wander Along the Beach Alone

I wander along the beach alone
And even in amongst the crowd
Tho dressed like they still I stand out
Still like an unwanted child am I
That longs to be no more -- outcast.

I join the others whom like I
From reaches of society all come
To roam within their kind and find
A place of peace and peace of mind
Still even there I walk alone -- outcast.

What cause in life condemns me
What penalty must I pay
What reason that I always feel
This deep loneliness always
Why yet must I remain an -- outcast.

But then my thoughts they flounder
My self-filled doubts are gone
It is not me that is outcast
But merely those a-passing by
For I have me a reason here
My life's with a purpose filled
My head's held high as I walk by
For I am master of my will
And that is why they treat me ever
... As Outcast

Life Is a Fire's Flame

Life is a fire's flame
Yesterday, today, tomorrow the same
Flicker, burn and onwards go
Shining out in useless glow

Love is like a fire's flame
A word, a feeling, a thought, a name
Yet one without the other's naught
And in this clasp we both are caught

Dreams that remind us of the past
Which were sweet and warm
Willingly we fulfilled each desire
Like the warmth of the glowing fire
So unlike these are you my love
That emptied my life it seems
Yet I hope that deep in dreams
One day you these will realize
Life and love and you alone
Each a part of my destiny
Each a need a feel within
So why why can't you realize
To me you're loves eternal fire.

It Was Summer's Ebb and Flow

It was Summer's ebb and flow
And one could feel the soft cold breath of Winter
Play upon the reaches of her warmth.

She came by in early Springtime
Dropped Winter's garb for cool scant Summer's wear
And like the Sun her body from flowed warmth.

Her lithe form yet uncovered
Save but for skirt short and blouse of sleeveless form
Her bronzed skin reflective of her warmth.

Upon her head of golden curls
Which fluttered down like feathers light
Upon her waiting shoulders
A net which seemed of spider weave there lay

As Summer's sun played its tattoo on her
While upon the deck she rested still that day
A solar blanket -- she -- enveloping suns warmth
Then Winter's long and cold and icy fingers
Reached out awhile 'neath safe shield of a passing cloud
To reach and touch deep within her warmth.

No move made she the moment for
No thought gave she to stay short the chill she felt
For so soon the sun returned with its warmth

Aye, but cunningly and cold Winter waited
Waited for the fall of Sun the last ray warm of day
Then fast returning she to capture
When eve had come, been and gone
When night upon the world did rule supreme

Here Winter's touch would be unhindered
Yet there she lay content still in her warmth
Enjoyment full in mind recalling warmth
Warmth of the late late Summer day.
Forgetful of the chill which she had felt.

Next morn a visitor dismal dark had she
One who calls but once each life within a trip to take
As there she lay in fevered warmth a-shaking
She lay in inner warmth extreme now so unwanted

To shake the chill of Winter's touch
She now no longer could
And as the Sun departed she did follow
To grace perhaps some greater warm surrounding

Or be companion constant
To the soft cold wintry winds
Or mayhap she to wait upon another
Another Springtime to in return again.

See My Love I Drop the Soap

See my love I drop the soap

Now that your hair has been washed

Let me now bend and wash your feet

That then I may them also cover with kisses

For of the body of the one I love

There is no part that I would not kiss

There is no part that I must not know

There is no part that remains a secret

For of the body of the one I love

This body I do love as my own -- completely

Remove the dust of the toil of day

Cleanse the proud sweat off thy brow

Lest all your former aches and pains

Like these that with the waters flow away

So too away from you let me them remove

For of the body of the one I love

There is no past haunting memories

There is no past hurt and agony

There is no cause to, to the past look

For I shall envelope you fully in love

For my love cannot be but a small portion

My love must encompass all that I love

For this is love -- true love -- love which lives

For of the body of the one I love

This body I do love even as my own -- completely

Yes this is love when no minute part

When no corner or secret of the other remains

But shared together they true one become

And this is the body which I love

From head to toe and all that's in between

This is the you which I see in me

As I become a part of you in love -- completely

If your parents had been normal like you,
you wouldn't be.
If it is a natural act
If it's an unnatural act
Let's see the two of you procreate
If you two are normal
then your parents were not
You can't be a real minority
if you made a choice.

The Tiny Pearl

Smooth crystallized teardrop
Embedded deep within the flesh
Like an ember in a flameless fire
Or a diamond's glitter in the night

So deep within the embryo of a shell
A snail-like creature without bones
A jelly-like protector gives you birth
Yet with its life you it e'er protects

You teardrop of such divine beauty
Which graces each place you enter in
You the desire of so worldly many
By your beauty which you e'er extend

Cultured, aye so you are and so called
Cultured thru the ageless years of man
Hidden ever in your watery haven
Ever sought to hold and to command

Teardrop, you a crystallized teardrop
But one weeping drop which crystallized
Hidden like a true deep deep treasure
Tiny Pearl -- hidden from the world

Like Liquid Amber Glow of Gold

Like liquid amber glow of gold
Which warms tho cold surrounding
Like the blood-red flow of wine
Which fills those it's encountering
Like the quench of thirst that's felt
As downwards flows the liquids
So too your very presence near
Fills the soul to overflowing

Then glance on and up awhile
Lend your smile to me a-short
Tho I may seem it to oft miss
But deep within it's ever caught
You, who lends light to the darkness
Suffer solace as friend to man
Share yourself so full unknowing
As you glance and smile again

Rose of the evening's Pub-light
Flower here among the thorns
Breath of fresh hope a-showing
'Til one day picked you will move on
Then like a candle's flickered ending
Light of this place it will have gone.

The Goose Has Flown Its Nest

The goose has flown its nest
And wide its feathers scattered
'Til each upright resteth on a log
Which floats upon the tide
And moving ever onwards
Across the seas they glide
In peaceful harmony with nature
Sails of the sailing boats.

One million wavelets lap the shore
One million notes are played
Each on a different harpsichord
As they the shoreline serenade
And I just sit in concert seat
And listen to the harmonious beat
As like a choir at my feet
Plays the ever-breaking waves
A drone of bass I hear afar
A plane a motor or a car
But then its sounds are drawn into

To mingle with or add anew
A chord so peaceful and so sweet
As ever onwards they repeat
The music of the tides and sea
Which seems to me a symphony.
Such peaceful tranquil majesty
Is often sought by nature's sea
When winds do blow the down-like sails
And push the boats across the waves

Tune in, turn up the orchestra
As listeners such as I walk by
To fill the stage and balcony
To sit in audience of the sea
As on the shorelines pebbles dark
The cacophony of sounds they start
Which mingles all with nature's sounds
To fill the hills and forests 'round

And then my heart like all the rest
Beats like a drum within my chest
As deep deep down within I hear
The music coming loud and clear
As there upon their curtain-less stage
They us their concert full parade
'Til naught else lives on but their song
Which goes on ever on and on
From whisper to triumphant clang
As the waves play music unto land.

The goose has flown its nest
And wide its feathers scattered
'Til each upright resteth on a log
Which floats upon the tide
And moving ever onwards
Across the seas they glide
In peaceful harmony with nature
Sails of the sailing boats.

The Beauty of a City A-Light

The beauty of a city a-light
Is like a bride prepared for bed
When viewed from a distant ship-side
While lingers Sun's parting rays of red.
The beauty of a city at night
With diamonds that twinkle and glitter
Is like a maiden that is to be wed
With her gown long and golden tiara.
The beauty of the city at evening
When its lights shows its beauty afar
Is like a woman in love contented
In whose face love radiates hard.
How then can one fault such beauty
Which spreads thru the darkness of night
Like love warm from a loving woman
It brings to the soul deep delight.
Each twinkle each sparkle each glitter
Like stars seems from heaven afar
Each building each bridge each roadway
Each house each boat and each car
Everyone is joining in symphony
Their concert of light to create
The beauty of the fair city so distant
Like a beautiful virgin she waits.

Glass Cutter Bow of Fishing Boat

Glass cutter bow of fishing boat
Which slice the mirrored waters
Which cut clear thru like diamond sharp
Against a piece of crystal
Disrupt you do the cutting edge
Yet untouched remains the other
Save for your crystal bits of glass
Which in your wake do follow.

Like knife upon a piece of art
Which cuts so carefully
It leaves the picture full intact
Save for the crease that be
No reverse art upon the glass
No paspateau remains the art
Full frescoed on the surface
As fishing boat you onwards ride
At slow steady, stubborn tide.

The hills around the birds above
The ship of noise which passes
These all reflect into the glass
As you alone sits quiet on it
Glass cutter bow of fishing boat
Heading home full and in leisure
Like artists brush your final stroke
Expounds nature's full beauty's splendour.

The Hunter

Bobcat or wolf or red fox
In distant view slowly appears
Then caught in the view of the eye scope
It's none other than white-tailed shy deer
Soft slowly one step sure it's taking
Ears upraised as it stops to check
Each flutter of leaves dry and falling
Sends shivers of fear to its depths
Then assured it will onwards again move
To the spot where the feeding is choice
But three steps at a time it taketh
Thereat pausing to check every noise
'Twix two trees now and feeling contented
Stops there but to feed for awhile
Unaware of the frozen stiff hunter
On whose rain-weary face breaks a smile
He the hunter six hours has waited
Thru the rain and the snow, wind and cold
For one chance but to capture his bounty

To feed his family thru long winter's cold
Not daring to breathe now he watches
Each step forward the shy deer it takes
Waiting for the right distance and moment
When one sure clean shot he will take
Up so slowly the rifle he raises

Up to his cold practiced eye
Then he reaches the cross hairs adjusting
O'er the spot whereto his bullet must fly
One sure shot's all he has for the taking
One clean kill with the shortest of pain
As his quarry he admires feeling sorry
But his family must be fed he thinks again
Two hundred plus fifty he figures
In pounds that thru winter will take
Good meals for the table left empty
No longer alas can he wait
Gripping so firmly the rifle
Breath held -- his finger caress
Feel the trigger respond hear the echo
A sure placed shot pierces the breast
Just two kicks gives the deer that has fallen
It is dead 'for he reaches the spot'
Tho remorseful he's proud that his quarry
Has been quick-killed with one well-placed shot

It is over the hunt and the waiting
Before him his winter food lies
Now he must fast complete preparation
While remains yet some light in the skies
Two hours later at last he can exit
Dragging his prepared catch behind
Heading homewards tired and weary

The agony of the kill yet on his mind
Soon his family looks upwards a-smiling
Glad they their meal table is graced
Unknowing of the hunter's deep sorrow
Of doing what he must this to face
'Tis not easy providing a living
When a life of a kind must be short
But no word of this ever he mentions
Just the luck of his one well-placed shot
Yet at night seems he sleepeth contented
For his body is tired and sore
But in dreams comes always a-haunting
That moment of death o'er and o'er
Still he'll face sad each season awaiting
Tho with seemingly eagerful pride
The time he his weapon can shoulder
To once more for his family provide

You -- youth -- inexperience,
Me -- age -- experience...
You -- exuberance
Me -- lethargy
Balanced perfectly enough
to harmonize our lives.

The Lion and the Scorpion

It was cold -- it was wet -- it was winter
The icy rain was sheeting off the bow
She was pacing the deck 'lone and aimless
Stopping to take pictures then and now
As she passed our eyes caught for a moment
Yet 'twas long enough for our souls to speak
Telling each the other felt just as lonely
Stranger -- yet so alike here on life's street
On she paced like a zoo caged wild one
Longing for spaces open and free
There in natures forest her true nature
Could forevermore roam forever free
Like Lisa she'd been tamed by a man's hand
Yet like Lisa for the wild still she craved
Deep within that urge came on unending
Beckoning from youth unto the grave
Kingly, Queenly a definite true royal
Stature full befitting of the best
Down suppressed roar groaned yet the echo
Which she longed and waited to express
Like the Lioness Lisa of Born Free
So she too had known rejection young
Grasping ever outwards for fulfillment
Often oh too often grasped she wrong
Is she wrong to seek her deep desires

When she knows they've never been filled
Is she wrong to haste out of the forest
Careless of the traps where she may be killed
Can one wrong this Lioness seeking shelter
Not protection -- for she herself is strong
Not a mate -- for she has had choices
Varied aye, and of scroll length full long
Nay one can but appreciate such beauty
When it's filled with strength and purpose clear
She alone must venture into life's garden
Seeking there the world for which she cares
Will she find her dream or go on dreaming
Will a hunter's shot first bring her down
Will she tired and injured lay death awaiting
Or drag herself up licking her wounds
Well alas -- this -- time alone can answer
All the questions 'neath her flowing mane
Shall she the past experiences turn bitter
Causing her to reach out in hurt and pain
This I doubt tho I'm a passing shadow
Whom upon her body short did rest
Lending solace to her lonesome moment
Feeling full the warmth of her caress
Like a wild once free caged Lion
Pacing endlessly 'round the cages walls
Knowing full the strength she possesseth
Knowing too its patience over all

Reaching out to help is also reaching
Reaching for a touch reciprocal
Strangers aye, we two now, no longer
Understanding she me understanding me her
Stay and ponder as your lair you wander
Look around the forests your domain
See the stump, the rock, the fallen pine tree
Under each you'll see perhaps my name
We both creatures of the free wild forest
We both searching for true peace and love
So unlike in makeup and appearance
Yet within, we two one has become
Travel on then Lioness to your forest
While beneath a ledge or rock I hide
We again in time will meet as this time
Me with new strength, you with a new found pride

Firm as iron,
soft as a breeze,
patient as time,
warm as sunshine,
clean as rain,
lovely as a tree --
you in all things I see

Red Winter's Gold Is Falling Soft

Red Winter's gold is falling soft
On yonder dusty mountain
Where spray of snow of yesterday
Soft lingers yet awhile
The moss green foliage of the trees
Surround it all encasing
The evergreens in clusters which
Stand to grace it all around.

Dark dismal silent without sound
Foreboding and forbidding
Protective mass of solid stone
A stones cast away doth seem
Ridged top like mountainous waves
Still ever on compelling
Reflecting full the Winter's gold
Cast from last rays of day.

The humble cottage blue and white
With silvered roof and windows
Which like a cool clear mountain stream
Sends sparkles everywhere
The standing Oak the towering Pine
Seems aback to be suspended
As to its solemn beauty
They too a part must play.

'Tis Winter's evening time again
But seems the snows have melted
Tho nip of cold remains outside
To crisp the evening air
The blue of sky is giving way
To soft grey shade of twilight
While high atop the hills and trees
Winter's evening Sun soft plays.

Red Winters gold on natures brush
Is passing swiftly onwards
As pensively I lay and watch
The scenes thru windows warm

The neighbour's humble cottage framed
Like photo of an old friend
Against the dark dark mountain
Reflective of the sprays of gold.

It's Winter's red red golden eve
The Sun's to rest departing
In peace with nature and the World
It's Winter's red red golden eve
Like life -- a day's departing
To wait and awake renewed
And remade whole.

<u>Mirrored Love</u>

You never say "I love you"
Like loving peoples do
But when I say "I love you"
"Me too" will echo you
(Does that mean you love you too)

You never reach to hold me
Or to be held in my arms
Yet when I reach to hold you
You nestle safe and warm

(Is this then but my warmth reflected)
You never think to kiss me
Or share first a warm caress
Yet if I try to kiss you
You return with warmth my kiss
(Or are my lips just pressed against my own)

You echo what I say to you
You mirror what I do
You never really give yourself
'Less first it's given to you
Like a reflective mirror
You in my image wait
Like a cold still shadow
You my every move imitate.

Where lies your warmth and feeling
Where hides your tender touch
I wonder this on endlessly
Since you mirror me so much.

How nice 'twould be to be held
When I didn't first you hold
How sweet a kiss to me receive
'Stead of but a kiss returned
To hear you whisper "I want you"
Without repeating just my words
To feel myself by you desired
While lying sleepy quiet secure

These things all mean I love you
In their own peculiar ways
The things you give and want and do
The things you clearly outright say
But when like a mirror you reflect
Or like a parrot my words repeat
They leave an empty doubtfulness
Of your love deep inside of me.

Mini-skirts prompted men to place women on pedestals

In Fields of Green Green Waters

In fields of green green waters
Which grasses are full swaying in the wind
I look and there thee I behold --
Besides the noisy brook
Which tries to whisper love words
More feeling unto thee than I --
Beneath the whispering willow tree
Whose mournful cry of loneliness
Would try my own to put to shame --
Bedecked in attire more picturesque
Than the singing birds around you
Who sing out warble words of love
In hopes to drown my manifestations --
But there I wait, I, among the swaying grasses
In silence there I sit,
And watch thee sit
I watch thee listen to the brook
And hear its words
I watch thee shed a tear
For the willows lonely moans
I watch thee cheerily join in song with the birds
Yet there wait I among the green green swaying grasses
Silent -- hidden -- alone and waiting
Waiting for I know well

Soon you will come a-gaily tripping

Carefree in answer to my hearts deep message sent

Then into arms, each other's,

We will for a stolen moment fall

Content in love for our moment

Our moment by time only lent

As we embrace, and love, and leave

Returning back to our separate worlds

You to yours of the rich and classy affluent

Me to mine of the poor, political malcontent

4/11/81

There Are Times When Life Is Gray

There are times when life is gray

There are times when life is sad

But I'll always remember those wonderful days

And the fun that we had

My darling you and I were walking

And watching the moon up above

I held your hand and whispered soft

Sweetheart it's you I love

Now I sit and hold that same hand

As my Sweetheart fades away

But I know in heaven she'll remember

I was with her 'til her dying day

I Come to the Sea Alone

I come to the sea alone
And gaze at the stars in the sky
Wondering while I glance at your picture
If you know why we said goodbye
I come to the sea all alone
Cause I have no one to call my own
Yet someday I know you'll return
And then you'll be mine all alone
I gaze at your picture both night and day
And wonder if it could be true
You said you are sorry in every way
And you ne'er more will make me blue

The Wretched of the Earth (English Version)

Wretched -- wretched
I seek peoples like myself
If there's one I cannot touch
Her I rape in spirit.
Wretched -- wretched
Wild with indignation
I to a fool may be compared
For this trifling little matter.
I will love if I am loved
As a man I like to live

She ignores my chatter.

Wretched -- wretched

Should I love if I'm not loved

Tongues I spurn that thrive on patter,

I seek peoples like myself

To turn to hatred's banner.

Wretched -- wretched

I seek peoples like myself

Speak my declaration

Brave in war -- Powerful in peace.

Wretched -- wretched

Father of the poor

Face to face with many a trial

Oft with danger's fraught.

Wretched -- wretched

I seek peoples like myself

Let our hearts beat gladly

Comrades let us drink.

Wretched -- wretched

Like a youth in mind

Down the highway broad I walk

To a flowing river

Bound by not a chain am I

Wretched -- wretched

I seek peoples like myself

Transient yet forever.

Miseros Terrae (Latin version)

Miserum -- miserum

Quaero populos mihi similes

Si quis contingere non est

Hanc ego stuprant in spiritu.

Miserum - miserum

Wild cum indignatione

Stultus ego comparetur

Hoc enim parvo materia.

Amabo, si diligor

Secundum hominem vivere amem

Illa ignorat mea loquacitate facturus.

Miserum -- miserum

Si veneror dilexit diligendus

Linguis, spernere ista laetatur CREPITO,

Quaero populos mihi similes

Ut transferrentur ad odium est scriptor vexillo donavit.

Miserum -- miserum

Quaero populos mihi similes

Meo loqui declaratione

In bello -- potens in.

Miserum -- miserum

Pater pauperum

Coram multis experimentis

Saepe cum periculo suus 'plenasque laborum.

Miserum -- miserum

Quaero populos mihi similes

Cor nostrum verberavit libenter

Conmilitones bibemus.

Miserum -- miserum

Quasi adulescens in mens

Down via lata ambulo

Ad fluviumque liquentem

Alligata non torquem sum

Miserum -- miserum

Quaero populos mihi similes

Caducae tamen in saecula.

The Foghorn

The foghorn failed at four in the fog

At four every forty minutes

The flogger was flogging fog-lights in the fog

If the foghorn stays foiled

'Til ten to four in the fog

How many fog-lights can the flogging

fog-light flogger flog in the fog?

(Answer on Page 99)

There Are Men Who Spend a Fortune

There are men who spend a fortune
'Tween a woman's scalp and toes
Trying to her fit into some scheme
With jewellery fashion and furs
Of high and expensive costs
They squander blindly onwards to their dream

There are women who pay tribute
To what they feel alone they own
Which somewhere 'tween the toes 'n' scalp doth lie
Some unique prize or treasure
Which no other mortal owns
Nor can own no matter how they try

There's a legend built on fantasies
Of the mysteries hidden there
'Tween a woman's feet and her topmost crown
Of the differences that linger
Unseen -- unreached -- unknown
For which many men have lain a good life down

Yet like a ship unpainted
All bodies are the same
And it's only what's within that matters most
The engine and accommodations
Which power and protect
And its stableness of which its sailors boast.

So waste not time in wondering
What treasures you may find
When among women you may walk as men
Just hold to short perspective
When she you scrutinize
Lay all your thoughts just 'tween her scalp 'n' chin

Then as your years run onwards
You her face will so oft see
In laugh, in pain, in sorrow or in pout
Yet thru it all some beauty there
Will hold you e'er enhanced
Playing on your mind somewhere around her mouth

For false lie all the fantasies
Which of women we men hold
Of bodies built fat, medium or thin
Apart from their chief attribute
Of a loving trusting heart
A woman's true loveliness lies
'tween her scalp 'n' chin

A person must feel wanted and needed before
they can accept the fact that they are loved

Teresa

Not of beauty's outer expose
Which of the world would rave
But inner beauty shining bright
Which all with free she shared
Like a diamond of the first sort
Set deep in precious gold
With many a rare and lovely stone
Supportively set all around

Like a rose among the thorns
Like a lamb among the sheep
Like a beaming light in dark of night
Like a dream in peace-filled sleep
She waits -- She waits, she waits
And all men say -- A Lady --

A Lady true she be
She carries forth her every worth
Full for the world to see
Her smile like Springtime falling
Upon a long chilled ground
Her eyes like evening's starlights
Glimmering in clear skies around

Her poise, her voice, her manner
Her movements each doth seem
An answer to man's visions
Of a living walking dream

Her gentile soft warm aura
Which around her all is seen
Setting her apart, in thought in heart
Like an untouchable star or queen

Yet proud she is not, surely,
Tho pride shines from her face
Aloof she wouldn't reach up for
Content to simply grace this place

Yet all who know or see her
Even when just passing by
Turn head in admiration full
She's a lady true -- they cry

Such innocence in maturity
Makes the world of men -- worthwhile
To feel the warmth she exudes
Each time she shyly smiles

Such inner beauty outwards cast
Is to mankind seldom given
As seen in this angels face on Earth
The Lady sent on down from Heaven.

Let God Walk These Hills With Me

Let God walk these hills with me
And speak in His many voices
To show me the way --
To live forth today --
As He would that I do from His choices
Let God take now my hand
And guide me His pathway along
Then place in my heart a song
To help me know right from wrong
Let God show His beauty to me
In each birds' song
Or leaf of each tree
In each song that the stream
Plays as it flows along
From icy snowfalls to sea
Let God walk these hills with me
Where He and I often talk
Where we alone may find or atone
For whatever He feels I've done wrong
Let God walk these hills with me
And speak in His many voice
Then I know I'll be told
How best to uphold
The standard of my living choices
For here in this temple of ours
Where the tall trees so worshipful wait

With their heads all held high
Praising God in the sky
While His care looking for to each day
Then teach me to be like the trees
As strong and as patient as these
That tho held to one place
Ne'er a frown on my face
Will I put there for what I've been given
Let God walk these hills with me
And speak in His many voices
Like the times in the past
Where His help I could ask
For each trouble that I didn't see
Let God walk these hills with me
And speak to me once again
Like Father to son our just one on one
But mostly just like a friend.

May life's waterfall
take your shoulders
for its mountain
spreading its rich gold
and its beautiful rainbows
around you for all your days

Come Up the Mountain's Path

Come up the mountain's path
And I shall meet you at the breakaway
To take thy loving hand in mine
And lead thee higher up in safety
Then we -- just you and I -- shall walk
Then we -- just you and I -- shall talk
Then we -- just you and I -- shall pause
Shall pause awhile in pregnant silence
-- And that silence it shall be mine
It shall be mine to tell thee I love you
It shall be mine to gaze in thine eyes
And without words speak loud yet to you
It shall be mine to whisper to heaven
How much beauty your face really holds
What a treasure lives in your curls
And what warmth in your arms enfolds
It shall be mine to mimic the songbirds
As they flutter from tree unto tree
Singing out loud love songs
Of love that never goes wrong
Love such as I have here for thee
And after our long pause of silence
When to you all these things have been told
We'll skip softly along
Thru the forest singing a song
And though I've not spoken yet you will know

Come up the mountain's path
Higher yet, lets up to the hilltop
Where the mighty trees all will seem
But twigs in a stream
As they're dwarfed by the river below
Then we -- just you and I -- shall sit
Then we -- just you and I -- shall think
Then we -- just you and I -- shall dream
Shall dream that it never will end
Shall dream we are now more than friends
Shall dream that all this is ours
Shall dream that nothing else matters
Shall dream that these times
Will return time after time
Each new day when you hear me say
Come up the mountain's path
And I shall meet thee at the breakaway
To take thy loving hand in mine
I lead thee ever high and higher

Wanton Desire
Free Abandon
Flaming Passion
Lost Inhibitions
are all links in the chain of a lasting love

Down the Trail from Mountain Pass

Down the trail from mountain pass
Where twilight shadows play
Where bluebirds chirp in melody
As throughout the rest of day
Down the trail from mountain pass
Where shy deer frolic yet
As evening sun her head sinks low
And day prepares for rest
Down the trail from mountain pass
Where ponies homeward trod
Without a care or worried thought
Their life all left to God
Down the trail from mountain pass
We slowly walk along
With memories of our mountain pass
Our thoughts go flooding on
Down the trail from mountain pass
We walk by stream and tent
We walk by fire with embers lit
With campers so intent
Down the trail from mountain pass
We see our journeys end
In face with smile that greets us there
And warm arms of an old friend

Down the trail from mountain pass
Thru timbers green and tall
We see life being yet full lived
We see them one and all
Down the trail from mountain pass
Where ferns in gardens wild
Do line the pathways of our trail
Brightening our trail on each side
Down the trail from mountain pass
'Tis twilight time again
And you and I must downwards go
We, hand in hand, as friend
Down the trail from mountain pass
Is easier than up hill
But each new day we tread e'er up
To our mountain pass yet still
For it is this the upwards climb
That at evening time gives worth
As down the trail from mountain pass
You and I at dusk sets forth

Women are largely E-motion and when
a man's around 'e gets 'em in motion

Come Sip the Mountain's Dew

Come sip the mountain's dew
The honey dew of mountain tops
Cool sweet first melt of snow
As Spring descends upon the land
And Summers future Sun peeps thru
Come sip come sip
Come sip the cool clear water
Like life giving youthful fountain
'Tis here thy troubles flee
'Tis here that truth and beauty
'Twill be given up to thee
Come sip come sip
Come sip the mornings sweet mist
As dew first here's collected
For it the new flowers kiss
Lending them its fragrance
Lending them its savour
Lending them as offered unto you
Its secret of its youth
Come sip come sip
Come sip the mountain fall stream
It's melting snows down trickle steadily
To cause a rivulet to form
To whisper soft among the sands
And create 'mongst the rocks a storm
Come sip from meadows fountain

Come listen as natures choir plays
Such a cacophony of mellow notes
Naught but the wilds could sing
Come sip come sip
Come sip then come sit awhile
Rest like a weary traveller
Who's traversed so many a mile
And here find you contentment
And here find you peace
And here find you true bliss
As natures fountain rolls along
To place on each stone a kiss
And you are more, much more
So much more than just a stone
That's why the fountain choir sings
A-loud out-loud for you it sings
That from its songs comfort springs
As you come sip from its cool waters

Climb the highest mountain
Dive the deepest sea
Written there thru ageless time
This message you will see
Today I LOVE YOU TRULY

Then Peace I've Found

If nature's sounds around me all be peace
Then Peace I've found
If nature's silence all me around be Peace
Then Peace I've found
If songbird's twitter in amongst branches be Peace
Then Peace I've found
If pause by timid deer to me gaze upon be Peace
Then Peace I've found
Yes Peace I've found here in these my forest hills
Where every sound is but an echo each of nature
Where wild meets wild and in that setting frolic
Where rustling leaves cause not a head to turn
As Peace is here and of it we have learned
If Peace be valley filled with heavenly song
Then Peace I've found
If Peace be cloudless skies from dawn to dawn
Then Peace I've found
If Peace be chatter light of a loved one's voice
Then Peace I've found
Yes Peace lives here within these hills of mine
For here my valley is filled with children's voices
And sun and stars stream endlessly down me on
While soft and gentle speaks the voice I love
Each but a tribute to the one above
And this is Peace, and this is Joy
And this is Nature's understanding
Thus Peace on Earth here I've found
As I pause here in these my forest hills

Oh Fountain of Youth, Truth and Beauty

Oh fountain of youth, truth and beauty

Let me share thy riches of Life evermore

Oh fountain of youth, truth and beauty

On my hands and my knees

I bow my head before God unto you

Oh fountain of youth, truth and beauty

I come to partake my daily sip

My sip of thy lifesaving stream

Oh fountain of youth, truth and beauty

I bend in reverence at thy banks

And list to the chorus of thy many voices of earth spring

I bend my ear to capture thy words of wisdom

I lend my thoughts to encapture

the truth you sing unto me

I bow in reverence unto our selfsame creator God

And as I bow, and as I pray

And as I kneel in His presence

Oh fountain of youth, truth and beauty

As I bend to sup of thy nectars

Grant with His powers your enchantment

Grant with His Grace your life

Oh fountain of youth, truth and beauty

A Symphony in Movement

Waves -- flowing, uncrested waves
Visible music
A symphony in movement
A symphony without a sound
A visible orchestrated rendition
Which only the eye can hear
Each beat, each bar each stanza
Each full harmonious note
Is writ not is played not
And yet on water's page
Each measure precise
Each rest, pause and quarter
In visible symphonic concert
Is being forever displayed
Waves yet not waves of water
For 'tis but water which they o'er flo
Total waves of music is moving
Moving moving ever moving
Like a celestial choir of angels
Like the voices of children in praise
They flow to surround and encapture
To thrill to move and enrapture
Each eye which rests them upon
Each eye which catches their beauty
As their soundless symphony plays
Plays on and on unending

Trilling the visions of watchers
As but to the eye its music it gives
Waves loud boisterous and foamy
Now cresting now rolling now gone
They too sing a song for the hearing
A song like the sirens of old
To capture man's imagination
To tear from him body and soul
Yet their music is heard by listeners
As they pass by awhile and are gone
But the silent music I'm seeing
In my mind's eye will live ever on
Waves soft slow quiet uncrested
Visible musical waves
A symphony in movement
A symphony in silence
A full symphony with nary a sound
An unending concertina flows down

Fair lady -- as a Black man
I woo thee not because
you are white
but rather in spite of that fact --
I woo thee.

Swishy Swish Splash Swishy

Swishy swish splash swishy
Trickle trickle trickle swish
Falls the water calls the water
Flowing onwards e'er like this
Close your eyes deep and wonder
Close your thoughts to all but sound
Hear the waters swishing splashing
Flowing o'er all rocks around
Tiny pebbles move and crackle
Boulder huge break the stream
Yet each one the water passes
Joins it seems the music's stream
Swishing splashing swishing splashing
On the marks of time it falls
There to lend harmonious echo
As it pure flows over all
Can't be hindered, stopped or held back
Can't by other be replaced
Cool and sweet clear yet fragrant
Odorless yet filled with taste
See the waters flow on forever
From rain to babbling brook to sea
Ever flowing wild and restless
Ever flowing wild and free

Lone Eagle

Lone Eagle
Sitting alone up so high
Are you alone by choice
Or by nature like I
Do you your home empty grace
Awaiting what seems ne'er to come
Are you but paying life's penalty
For being so forceful and strong
In your quest for steady companion
What did you meet on the way
That cause you to soar to the high peak
Away from the crowds all to stay
Lone Eagle
Lone by nature or choice
Or by beyond your control circumstance
You still can fly to your destiny
You still can seek a new chance
You Eagle blessed by solitude
Wherein at least peace you find
Soar on ever on oh lone Eagle
On your wings ride hope yet of mine

Work is an invention to assure married peoples
a few hours of happiness each day

Smog

Smog

A fog-like cloud

A dense suspended smoky haze

Like a bond of burnished copper

Around the seaside hills it hangs

Draped like a careful placed memento

Like an amber band of condemnation

It stays each day at evening

'Til the light of day is gone

Then softly slowly

Like the distant clouds

Like a nesting bird of night prey

It rises slowly upwards upwards

Then in the darkness disappears

Smog

Some more of our garbage

Our great air killing waste outspun

From cars, industry and planes

Our residue of an affluent society

Which everything around it tries to change

Unmindful e'en as we the haze create

That this soft copper-like smoky cloud

Will one day us envelope and our lives abate

Annihilate

You're Dying Kelsey Bay

Dying you're dying Kelsey you're dying

You're dying and soon you'll be dead

Like the derelict hulls that a-front you

Which from waves anger protected

Which were built for nations protection

Which now lie rusty and solemn

Which now lie rotting before you

Which now lie dying and dead

So too you're dying Kelsey you're dying

Soon but a train stop you'll be

Soon but a smoldering lumber yard

Soon but a port near the sea

A port which has been open free

A reminder of past industry

Now gone now dying alone you

Now but a name that'll remain

A name in recall of past fame

Each time a ships whistle blows

Each time a boat cross by goes

Your left faithfuls they will know

That Kelsey you're dying you're dying

Like the derelict hulls that a-front you

You're dying and soon will be dead

Uncapturable Beauty

Such uncapturable beauty
Which the eyes alone behold
As enter and exit each
Fjord-like passageway we pass
Like Jason's clashing rocks
Of monstrous weight falling
Falling on the unsuspecting traveller
Here too we gaze they upon
But fall apart they never do
Firm and majestic they remain
To beautify each turn we take
To grace with splendour full
Each seemingly unopened route
As into sheer blank mountainside
Each timber laden hilly slope we wander
In quest are we our itinerary to complete
Another voyage make into oblivion
But part they do and we pass on
Betwix the seem impassable terrain
To gaze back as together they once more
Will form anew their unbroken chain
And leave us speechless silent gazing
At such un-capturable beauty

You Stand Alone???

You stand alone???
Ah yes, I stand alone
So too the soaring eagle
Which drift from crag to crag
In search it seems of solitude
In search of peaceful serenity
His nest a mass of cutting
With sharp protective edge
High, high upon the topmost tree
Which grows tall from highest hill --
Is this a right to self-preserve
Or just a quirk of inner fear
Who questions him his wisdom
Who dares his private world invade
And as he soars so high above
Majestic he his call all others fear
And so tho peace filled and unwavering
In his own solitude he revels
Constant in his never changing knowledge
That he who would respectfully be held
Must like the stars and Gods themselves above
Hold in abeyance the mystery of Himself
And be content to stand it seems alone

The Golden Sun

The last brush of gold it falls
Upon the far horizon
And Natures golden sun once more
Disappears for night to fall
Solemn grey clouds above sit
The mirror-like waters wait
Each to be enhanced so by it
As they're touched soft by its paint
A ribbon road of reddish gold
Sent out to each that views
Across the rolling waters
Accentuating full their blues
Each dark grey cloud a lining
Of silver and gold is given
To show their worth in picturesque scene
As they sail across the heavens
Then as the pot of gold moves down
Just a sheen is left to view
As you take your gold and move along
My heart, Sun, it goes with you.

Making love may sound so beautiful but
only hard hot wet passion will satisfy

The Water Falls...

As the cool cascading waters fall
In rushes down the tall hillside
To smooth the rock
To grow the trees
To feed the flowing river
Tho white and foaming billowlike
Controlled it flows and falls forever
As nature's rain fall soft upon
The warming melting snows
The birds seek bits of food afloat
The beast lair and shelter knows
In nook and cranny and in cave
Which the waters once rushed o'er
And far below the silent sea
Waits its salty thirst to quench
As the residue cascades and falls
Down o'er all therein to end
The stream and rivulet is fed
The trees have grown and blossomed
The rocks are smooth which jagged were
'Fore the waters flowed fast o'er them
And still it flows from mountainside
In cold foamy white cascade
To grace the land to touch the seas
And the rivers wide to feed.

Where the Sea Porpoise Play...

Out where the gulls and the sea porpoise play
Frolicking across the still waters
O'er the deep current swells
O'er the blue waters crest
O'er all the tides and the seas
Banks of clouds land like a picture creates
Framed by the sky and the sea

Painted-like fish boat and tugboat and yawl
Seems not to move in their wake
But so slow spreading
T'wards new borders turning
So softly it's reaching it seems
For a unity to form and as one become
Like a deep sleeping dreamer in dreams

Then the gulls flash high their wings overhead
While the porpoise lends a display
Top swimming then jumping
In waters crystal and clear
Thru the gossamer sea and the air
In groups they like children in play out at school
Swimming free they swim happy in pair

Against the cloud backdrop like a cold lonely ghost
A distant distinct ship is seen

Far across the mirror-like waters
Where the sea porpoise play
Like a vision paint captured it lays
Snug nestled in frame of the sky and the sea
'Cross the place where the sea porpoise play

<u>Nature's Child...</u>

As the first cold winds of winter blows
The dark clouds seem to settle low
Around the crest and baldy tops
Of the mountains awaiting snow
As the kiss of cold turns green to gold
And the trees shed the leaves they hold
In prep for weight upon their limbs
When they endure falls icy cold
The birds a new coat of warmth
Builds soft beneath their feathers
I sit alone and watch the winter enter
Making cold the world outside
Once more a part of nature now I feel
For cold inside am I since you did leave

Let not thy life be ruled by overt passion
let not thy love leave seeking it

Celestial Beauty

Come thou celestial beauty

Let me feed from thy forests

Let me sup from thy lake

Let me worship full thy sky

Less time which now is passing

Unfulfilled may pass us by

Like flowing limbs of summertime

Which fragrance filled with flowers are

Whose leaves hang down inviting warm

Your hair like a forest seems

Deep smooth calm and peaceful

Still blue like heaven's reflections

Like warmth of wine you call me

When of thine eyes beauty I partake

Then music sweet flows round me

Enveloping fulfilling

Like sirens song of ages past

My head in giddy fashion swims

This then is but thy music
As rosebud lips rest open
And words cascade in harmony
From an angels repertoire
Celestial bells start ringing
Heavens own choir is singing
While I stare unbelieving
At all that to me you are

Come then thou celestial beauty
Let me feed free from thy forests
Let me sup full from thy lake
While I worship in thy sky
Let me live among the Gods abode
Tho it means I then must die...

When Sex becomes Love
When Lust becomes Desire
When Want becomes Need
When Dirty becomes Clean
It is simply because
You are in my thoughts

The Fine Art Critic...

You are an artist true she said softly
And I in reply could only 'thank you' mutter
Yet I knew full such ecstatic pride today
Such as each worker in the arts seek so long after

For here a lady fine and cultured
One wise and well acquainted
With the finest of fine arts
One high acclaimed and treated e'er with dignity
Her opinion sought and valued thruout the world of arts
And she this lady had a moment taken
My attempts to view and speak on in honestness
And I in my attempts my art to further
Here had so deep her interest held and she impressed

Then to that mental state so many hope for
That euphoric heavenly reach there in the mind
I'd soared and soared and soared beyond my understanding
To reach
To enter in
And joy 'twas mine

So simple it seems the artists ultimate
Their goal but this reach once to attain
To hear the world proclaim
You are an artist truly
Confirmed in words by one of such art fame

I've crawled, I've walked, I've run,
I've reached for heaven
I've dreamed, I've hoped, I've planned
It seemed in vain
But today,
Today I've reached arts highest hilltop
Yes you're an artist true she said
Followed by my name...

Do You Remember the Day

Do you remember the day when
Elmer got Tippe, Ann Lost and
Pam Hurt watching an embarrassed
and Red Robinson trying to
get Dave's Cash back from Daves
Brown houseboat which fell off
of Roys Jacks which Diane'd
Given to Campbell who was
a-coming to say that Bob Buys
Jims Fraser river stories from
Ken Neds SuperCountry Peacock
farm where the fishing line of
Ted Pecks away at the Waltsnappers
which would rather Ford
the creek than the Rivers

Ode to a Woman's Breasts

Gaze I upon thy pair of sirens soft,
Semi-sphere-like sisters that emotions raise
Wed to each other one yet still apart
Living entities so enveloping my gaze
Long life their call unto me was heard
Their coo-like soft and silent sounds
Draw fast like nest doth draw the bird
When Winter's o'er and Natures Spring's in the air
Two sisters -- twins -- of simple parentage
Each compliment of the other rest
So soft yet firm they stay suspend
By taller half than their supportive tree
Mankind thee tribute to shall every pay
In words -- in song -- in looks and rhyme
In touch -- caress of feather soft
In respect for early nourished time
In gratitude for thy young which there
Doth hold their heads and in comfort feed
In love they warmth to feel pressed near
As at the pillars -- favours for they plead
Oh sirens of Natures softest bower
Thy songs to mankind all is known
No breath 'twas kept into a life
Which first was not a breath thy own
No step upon the face of Earth
Has yet made man with thee unknown

Thy semi-spheres his infant recollects
Which on he lay like king upon a throne
Gaze yet doth I and man in awe
Each time twin sisters pass us by
Their secret silent song calls softly out
Like eerie sirens in deep passions cry
Woman thy pillar and thy tree
The post where from you do hang
Thy refuge from the wiles of weak
Hungry -- searching -- Unscrupulous Man
Let rest within thy calm protective nest
Thy semi-spheres of loves first delights
Pulse by the heart which beats beneath
Causing hearts to quicken at thy sight
Twin sisters thee of Natures silent bower
Thy call to man like siren song goes out
Thy reach extends all man to o'erpower
As soft
-- innocent --
-- and free --
you dance about...

In times of illness and despair
collect the silver of the Sun
or the gold of the Moon
and share them with someone who's blind

Last Night I Dreamed

Last night I dreamed that I was home
And raced in boat across the gossamer waters
Watching all the tall reflective coral shoals below
Then I awoke with heavy heart and I cried

Last night in dreams I drove again the roads
Where as a young and happy man I'd roamed
Where friend along the wayside waving waited
And my soul was filled to bursting at the sight

Last night my thoughts became again realities
As back again in time my body lightly raced
Back to the childhood of my happier days
Back to my calm and simple island place

Along the reef where green waves pounded
Against the wrecks all torn by summer storm
O'er all the fish which swam so clearly
In waters flowing o'er white coral sands so warm

Last night as I dreamed my heart it light became
My thought of lost hope and of deep despair
Had for the first of many years me left
And I was happy once like my youth

Last night my soul a journey back did take
My being full thru the ages past did race
To stand again beside my kith and kin
And laugh in joy again seeing my glad father's face

But I awoke and it was gone from me
I came back to life's grim realities
And my sad heart it filled and o'erflowed
Then once again inside of me I cried

Yes last night I dreamed again that I was home
My broken heart renewed with laughter filled
My aches of years were so peaceful and still
Then I awoke and with heavy heart I cried

Fear Not

Fear not the night of darkness

Fear not the loss of light

Fear not the silent stillness

Fear not, my love, fear not

I shall be there besides you

To brighten up your night

I like a burning candle shall

Be to your dark a light

I shall the silent stillness break

With words proclaimed of love

That you may rest assuredly

And fear not, fear not my love.

300693-3

Hey J...

Hey J walk away from me
Into yonder fields of clover leap
Into beds of flowers with perfume
To grace and sweeten full your every step

Hey J walk out of my world
Having brightened full some hours few
Having my thoughts race on so free
A-galloping along with hopes on you

Hey J step lively now as you go
Proud straight and upright hold thy head
Your eyes aglow your hair of auburn red
Lingers warm as alone I lay instead

Hey J in your own way softly speak
In your wordless messages of deep thought
Each word so loud and clear to easy read
As a tremble smile plays about your mouth

Hey J once on you a fortune I amassed
As you outran the stallion foal and mare

But now it seems my last wager all is lost
For tho you try no more can you compare

Hey J your beauty still is fair to see
From sheen of coat to shiny polished shoe
Your rest deserved is envied not by me
As in your clovered field I watch you go

Hey J run on your time's been spent
Our race is o'er and stand the loser I
Yet as I watch you walk silent away
I fain would bet another time to try

Hey J run on you lovely girl
Your body young vibrant lithe and warm
Run on across the perfumed fields of clover
But first rest once more your head against my arm

Most times a ladies "NO"
is silently proceeded
by "I really don't"

If Only You Could Know

If only you could know
How much you are loved
And how little it is felt
As being returned by you
If only you could dream
The visions of love I hold
And the fantasies I'd share
If I only could but reach you

If only you could feel
The loneliness I live
The emptiness the longing
To be held and you to hold
If only you could know
How much you are loved
How much you are loved
By me in every way

Then and only then would you
See across the shadowy waters
Thru the deep mind blanketing fog
Which keeps our souls apart

Then and only then would I
Lose my empty lonely feeling
Which surrounds my very being
When you're not by my side
Inside I feel you near me
In thoughts I kiss your lips
Your body's warmth envelops
Removing all my chills
My dreams become realities
My fantasies are alive
My life has found a meaning
Which your presence here fulfills

If only you could know
How much silently I love you
And how fearful it is feeling
It may not be returned by you...

Swim not where thou fish
Less you increase to thyself
The danger of sharks.

"Pledge of Love" (1)

Oh give to me the right to be

that which I desire

To live and share

To hope and care

To love you ever higher

To do the things which life so far

Has from our paths removed

To say the words which until now

Remained silent -- unsaid -- unmoved

============

Oh give to you the time to live

To fulfill your choicest dream

To see your every hope and plan

Become a reality

To see you smile and hear your voice

Like an angels chorus fall

Free, fearless and forevermore

Upon my ears with love

============

Oh give to us the right to live

To be that which we choose

To bring as little or as much

Into our lives secure

To have the strength to work each day

To provide our means of life

To have the patience and fortitude

To enjoy and love thru life

============

These things we ask as we now join

Our hearts and hands as one

The right to live, love and be free

Thru each new days last Sun

Until our lives begin to ebb

And our lifes Sun goes down

Then may we walk 'long hand in hand

To our last purple dawn

To seek, to find, to want, to care

To be one as now we be

Forever joined thru all our days

I pledge this my love to thee

"Pledge of Love" (2)

When morning breaks the sun comes up

The light of day is seen

There comes again full warm to me

My thoughtful, hopeful dream

I see the Sun on mornings dew

I hear the birds sweet singing

But o'er it all I see the love

In eyes I sit beholding

I see the eyes so soft and warm

My being it seems embraced by

I see the lips I've kissed this dawn

And for many dawns long gone by

I see the face which close to mine

Breathes life anew for living

I see the strength for my days toil

There in your words unspoken

I look within the realm of your heart

And like a crystal mirror

I see myself there living safe

Locked by your charms forever

And then when I return again

To outward life and living

I see your warm and welcome arms

So open warm inviting

I enter into ecstasy

As to myself I draw thee

Feeling your sweet tenderness

As you snuggle warm against me

Then Darling is there any doubt

Or cause that you should worry

You I cannot live without

To lose you I'd be sorry

So as the day begins to break

And as I draw you near me

It's really to recall to you

All that you have meant to me

And as I hold you in my arms

I rise up to heaven above

It's here I hope you'll ever stay

My one -- sweet -- warm Precious Love

Olde Baldy...

Olde Baldy... Mountainous there you lie
In majestic splendour and beauty
Your foot firm planted on the land
Your head above touching the sky
The eagle bald and highly soaring
Will not today your height pursue
For on your summit rests the nest
Built by him on your loftiest view
Olde Baldy... Lie you silently there
While man and time itself rolls by
Your blouse of sun kissed fairy-feather clouds
Your skirt a forest green and gold as we pass by
High silent and unmoving yet constant
Save but by the sky itself your beauty unsurpassed
From dawn of the universes beginnings
'Til end of time you doubtlessly will last
So clean and bald you your head yet upholding
Soft waiting for the wig of winter's snow
Then in new gown and shawl you'll be showing
Your supreme majesty to all who by you go.

Bind tightly thy love and watch it leave hold loosely
thy love and it will forever with you abide

Memories of You

The glimmer of the moonlit night departs
As mornings sun beats down in shining hue
The glitter of the snow shines on the grass
As I sit and reflect on my memories of you
The dark and dismal mountain stands high
Bedecked atop with the morning lights
White capped with snows of the times gone by
It holds its head upwards thru day or night
Alas the gleam of day brings to ones eye
The soft and gentleness of the wavy sea
The outlines of the few birds which fly
E'er onwards o'er the lonely lonely sea
'Tis then my thoughts they go a-wandering
To times and places and to friends I've known
To distant lands across far warmer seas
To where a heart could live on with loneliness gone
I pine inside for things that must not be
I try but cannot now recall those days
I live in make believe a life of fantasy
On this lonely sea in a cold and lonely haze
Trying to forget the memories of you
Really trying to forget the fond memories of you

"Notice even the sweetly singing songbird
is strangely quiet once its nest is filled with eggs"

"That Just Loved Look"

How long have you had it
Where did you find it
How did you capture its glow
What gave it to you
In your innocent ways
That look each man seeks to know
Why is it that you unknowing possess it
When it every man thru life tries to find
And still so unaware
You sit there with it
That full 'just loved look' in your eyes
That look that to man means contentment
If it but once on his woman appears
Tells him she's truly happy to be there
Removes all his doubts and his fears
That look that says
She's his completely
Part laughter part pleasure surprise
That glowing 'just loved look' of wonder
Which shines so full from your eyes
That look which the face full envelopes
Like a blush that refuses to leave
Letting lips full and tempting rest open
As if the bearer is too happy to breathe
The short gasp-like breaths that go with it
Like an "Ahhhhh" so soft from the mouth

The slight tremble of chin
Tho held firmly
All extend the look beautiful out
One then cannot but ask in wonder
Being you this look constantly share
What Goddess blessed you with its presence
Placing that 'just loved look' on you there
This heart rejoiced just to see it
While others for you envy bear
For they wish like you they could capture
That 'just loved look' that you wear
Alas but to few it is given
To cast even their eyes long upon
And that's why when you they see glowing
They look upon you it seemeth in scorn
Those looks tho are but fond admiration
And respect for what they see there
To satisfaction true goes ever their tribute
To you and that 'just loved look' that you wear

Life is a fact;
Murder is killing after the fact,
Contraception is killing before the fact
and thus
Abortion is killing during the fact

Love Lives On Forever

Love Lives On Forever

It is Fearless

It is Endless

It is Faultless

It is Indestructible

It is all Giving

It is all Encompassing

Once we have loved we never stop loving

It is the fool who says 'love has died'

It is the fool who says 'I have lost love'

It is the fool who says 'I have fallen out of love'

Love is without bounds, -- without shame -- without

vengeance -- without the capacity for jealousy

Love sees not its carrier

but only those whom on it is bestowed

Love then is the ultimate form of expression

-- the ultimate compliment --

the ultimate goal of all living things

Love is eternal and thereby eternity

Love is God and thereby God is love

Love is boundless

Love is healing

Love is comforting

Love is warmth

Therefore love is the only true-lasting

-- honest expression of life

To have loved is to have lived

and to have lived is to have known love

Life -- breath -- existence are all

but the by-products of love expressed

Who then can say I am unloved

Who then can say I never knew love

Who then can say I cannot love

Who then can say I will not love

Only the Fool

For be it large or small

Be it good or bad

Be it right or wrong

Be it whatsoever it may

Only the fool rejects the one ultimate gift given to all --

Only the fool disallows the existence

of the elixir of life itself --

Only the fool shuns LOVE...

Strange... the ignorance and uncouth
behaviour of man is made most manifest
under the influence of alcohol or
in the presence of a beautiful woman.

The Virgin's Demands

A fit and aging bachelor

Once marriage entered on

Yet never willing was he

To leave his life of fun

He'd hoped to have his woman

Kids and wife and home

An occasional thing or mistress

Quite like he'd always known

So a young and virgin lady

'Twas on he made his play

Unsuspecting of her cunning

Evermore to have her way

"Sweet love of life"

She called him, "Come

Sit here by my side,

I want and need and love you"

This way she him did chide

"You know I feel my Darling

To give you my best my all

But scared am I remembering

Past hearts which to you called

I ache and burn my desire

For you does stronger grow

'Til I no longer trust myself

Still I cannot yet let go

For if I release my honour

And have you walk out on me
I'd've lost my only treasures
No more will good men seek me
That's Darling why I say no
Tho so deeply you I want
But come hold, kiss caress me
But stop, stop you know I can't."
The challenge had been entered
Accepted in full store
This untouchable morsel
He must make his now sure
So thinking on the reasons
She had to him laid down
He polished his excuses
Her defenses to tear down
"My love you know I love you
I have done since first we met
You haunt my days and sleeping
In life you are my breath
'Tis true I've been a roamer
Had ladies far and near
But they to me were passing ships
None with you could compare
Each of them gave their favours
In return for what they sought
Then tiring of their conquest
Left me with empty heart

'Til I in desperation
Did make a solemn vow
I'd seek a true and honest girl
To share with everlasting love
And heaven in its wisdom
Touched light for me your heart
You're all I'll ever want dear
Say from me you'll never part
My life it would be empty
Without you to help fill
Your wants my wants forever
Your dreams my hopes to fill
Your desires each one taken
Molded to full reality
I want and need and love you
Throughout far eternity
So Darling if you feel best
To withhold yourself awhile
I'll understand and patient wait
'Til we walk down that aisle."
Thus was it that his plan
Was laid in fullest style
For weeks and months she waited
Him a firm date to decide
Each time they met
Each date she'd set
He'd change or suspend

Yet faithfully at each meeting

He'd once more make a play

Still stop short she would put him

Until their wedding day

'Til in final desperation

He proclaimed "Okay today today

I can wait love no longer

Let's go do it all today

Grab your coat and bag

Your hat and other things

I've the license in my auto

In my pocket are your rings"

"Okay Darling I am ready

So long I've waited true

No more to be afraid here

To give full myself to you

And happy love we shall be

As man and wife we live

Your wants and mine united

As love we to each other give."

Down to the place of marriage

They drove and nervous stood

'Til the man pronounced them married

Forever thru bad or good

Then off in joy and laughter

They spent their honeymoon

They seemed so very happy

The time passed by so soon
'Til pregnant in her sixth month
She out of shape became
Then somehow now this woman
To him seemed not the same
She did not change he admitted
But life had become routine
He longed to enter in the chase
Of life's hunts of loves schemes
So calling an old acquaintance
He plans made to go see
Unaware that she had listened
The other phone on carefully
"My Darling" now he told her
"Tonight I may be late
There's work yet to be finished
Don't for me dinner wait
I'll grab a shake and burger
If perchance I get the time
'Tween catching up the office at
An' servicing that car of mine."
She kissed him ever sweetly
Knowing well that he had lied
But having planned so carefully
For this when it he tried
"Don't worry love it's okay
I know you've lots to do

I'll have some extra time now
To catch up on things here too
And I may even take the time
To visit or call a friend
It would be nice to see some
Of our old friends once again."
He left the hours ticked by
'Til ten to four drew nigh
Then leaving fast the office
He in his car did fly
Six miles then off a side street
To an old familiar house
Without a knock he entered in
As quiet as a mouse
Then thru a jarred door nearby
Which to a bedroom led
Dropped softly by the woman
Who lay unclad upon the bed
"It's been so long my lover
Since last you came around
I thought you'd forgotten me
Or that you had left town
It's nice tho to be seeing you
And have you here awhile
I'd almost forgotten 'bout your wife
How sweetly you still smile."
And ten past four

Just eight blocks down
A woman sets out from home
Polaroid and a paper typed
She held beneath her gown
Then to a house so silently
The window she stopped by
Took fast ten shots on camera
Of two people who did lie
Then taking one she hid the rest
A distance safe away
And quietly returned to
Where the two still lay
Then softly entering the door
She stood so lovely framed
Took deep a breath to anger still
"John -- Jane" she called their names
They sprang upright sat frozen
As beneath her gown she held
Her hand firm on the papers rolled
While each thought they were dead
"Don't move or talk just listen
To what I have to say
I hoped and prayed I'd never
This scene have to ever play
Still I in anticipation
Seeing what had been before
Felt insecure for reason good

Living near this your private whore
So long ago I entered all
The things I would demand
From any infidelity which
Was dealth me by my man
And then while still unangered
I could sit and clearly think
I'd written each in statement form
Copies three with pen and ink
So sit still as I read them
Then all each of us will sign
One copy each receiving
Outlining demands all of mine
And failing in this venture
I've pictures hidden nine
Which would break you John forever
Your husband's reputation by you
Jane no more you'd find
'We the undersigned do agree
That to... whom we did wrong
Me John by being husband unfaithful
Me Jane by knowingly going along
Knowing both we are married
Yet choose to our favours share
Unthinking of our spouses we
Whom for us deeply care
On this date at this time we

Did with each other lie
In infidelity and lust
Our passions to satisfy
And having been discovered
And seen our pictures taken
We swear to be forever true
If we now are forgiven
But should I John or Jane
Evermore these chances take
Be it together or apart
This contract we shall break
And public then releasing
The pictures and this note
You'll have the right to with it
Full restitution to evoke
We promise mere never again
To seek out as company
Each other while still married
To our spouses yet are we
We swear to be full faithful
Truth-filled and honest too
To never breathe a word of this
To anyone about you
To protect your name and marriage
To assure your happy life
To leave you free of worry
To respect you as John's wife

To leave your options open
Should one vow here go astray
To collect in full at anytime
For these infidelities today'
These then are my demands
My wants and dues in full
Now if you'll both just sign
He and I out of here will pull"
"We'll sign, we'll sign, don't shoot please
Forgive us if you can
Thank you for giving us this chance
Forever he's your man"
Thus was it that the virgin
Did break her wanderer
From his philanderings
From all his gad-abouts
And married happy she remained
He faithful did learn to be
Which proves the best laid
Plans of Man
Woman foils by matrimony...

Sex is not an act
as an act is a staged performance
but rather a physical psychological
shared fulfillment by mature beings

The Past Is Gone the Future Lives...

The past is gone the future lives
Look back not these upon
We've lived our lives in hurts and pains
We've shared them everyone
You've known your share of hurts and aches
You've had your bitter life
You've had your years of haggaring being
As the lonely unloved wife
You've had your days of turmoil spent
With lovers cruel mean
Forget the past the future looms
Let's live out now our dreams

Forget the past the future looms
Cause me not back to glance
I too have held life's lonely pains
The broken false romance
I too have shed the lonely tear
Heartbreak and sorrow known
I too have sang the empty song
That cold blue and lonely one
I too have had the mate who stood
Besides my side alone
Tho there in body not in mind
Nor soul... and ne'er my own
I too have known the bitter strife
I too have seen the hate
Forget it all the past is gone
But life's future for us waits

The future there so bright ahead
Is waiting shining there
As clearly as the smile upon your lips
Brightening full your face... so fair
As bright as your eyes which shine
So full of love there in your face
More love and hope than e'er yet seen
Upon a mortals face
The future bright it lies ahead
Be it 'twix or 'tween we two
We each can to the other lend
Some cared moments shared with truth

We two can share each other with
A moment short... of love
A moment which we often will
Speak oft so fondly of
The future full looms ahead
Speak then of love and life
Speak of happiness fulfilled
Speak now of all things bright

Speak no more of dark past days
Speak no more of hurt-filled years
Come wrap your arms around me love
Let me kiss away your tears
The past is gone and dead
So let it rest fore'er
The future full lies out ahead
For you and me somewhere...
Somewhere...

When Last Have You Sat

When last have you sat and watched

The painting of the skyline

As morning sunrise spreads

Upon the World its rays of reds and gold

As birds fly low o'er waters calm

As e'en the wind lies silent

Awaiting but another day to see unfold

The mountains dark like shadows

The wisps of clouds so scattered

The ripples and the wavelets

All wait with bated breath

The paint of nature's sunrise

The colours of a morning

A scene such as once seen

A heart can ne'er forget

The pattering of the ship

As on its ways it goes

Seems but the only moving thing

Which stirs the beauty round

But rather than taking away

Its movements but add splendour

To give to all the viewers here

Such a panoramic display

So softly now the few clouds all

Have gained their silvered lining
Whilst 'neath their far reflections
The sheets of gold appears
Then o'er the distant waters
And 'tween the hills and mountains
The beauty of the dawn... breaks...
Flashes red and gold-like
Fill every small dark corner
As the morning sun appears.
Ah, such beauty is so seldom
And e'en more so seldom
Such beauty it is seen
For few, too few, far, far, too few
Will take the time from sleeping
On a calm day to rise and wait
To see the new days begin
So cool tho it may be in winter
Yet warm one feels within
If thought is given to nature bright
Ah, its splendour it's a-showing
A new day bright has broken
In seconds spent but few
A long and lasting memory made
Watching the early morning Sun
Break through.

Say Not Any Word to Any Man

Say not any word to any man my lad
Unless you're certain it before in your mind you had
Do not anything to any man my son
Unless you realize it's what you feel
certain must be done
Ask no one to be below you subordinate
Let no one ever hold you so
Nor against you discriminate
Remember we each were born
Free men upon this land
And each must strive to protect these rights
In every way He can
Sometimes you'll find by doing so
You'll lose for just awhile
But seeing some other prosper
Will put on your face a smile
So do not worry if today
Seemeth dark and grey
If you know you've done your duty son
Soon it will pass away
But darker still will be the one
Who discriminated against you in a hurry
While brighter 'twill be your life
And for it you won't be sorry
Examples such as I have set
Among these friends and foes of mine
Will be re-enacted when these things they've met
Which now are considered faults of mine

As Summer Leaves

As I feel the soft breath of summer pass me by
I hear the echoing echoing beat of every heart
this summer met
Of every turn this summer took
Of every tear this summer shed
I, without you, without you
As summer passes and gives way to Autumn's cold
And long nights and short wintry wintry wintry days
And there is naught, naught in my mind
Of places where one visits and places yet to go
Where peace and quiet one can find
As summer goes, as summer leaves
And, yet I sit, I sit and watch as summer leaves
as summer passes by
Yet here I sit feeling the last warmth of summer's sun
All I know is of winters cold and freezing ragged breath
And I for far warmer climes I yet do yearn
As summer leaves, as summer me passes by
And winter's cold, cold breath is felt upon my face
As summer, as summer leaves, as summer
Leaves and passes me, passes me by

September 22, 2011

What more can I say
On your Special Day
Than 'I Love You'

The Bare Uncut Diamond

Since last that I held you softly
And near to this body of mine
My thoughts think of naught but the kisses
You lay on me like sweet cherry wine
My arms reach for you while I'm sleeping
My voice keeps loud calling your name
My dreams filled with the remembrances
Of when together these things we'd share
I walk along the streets of Chatterley
With life and future in thought
A picture of your face e'er before me
Saying without you my life is for naught
I vision a lifetime of rapture
A release from my past lonely toil
I see a fulfilled lasting moment
As fore'er life with you I enjoy
'Tis then that my feet ceased their travel
'Tis then that my eyes were affixed
As I gazed in worshipful wonder
Like a love-stricken fool so perplexed
Before me lies naked such beauty
Which with you alone could compare
In beauty, in culture, in majesty
A diamond unmount, uncut, lying bare
It seems that a glow hung thereover
As your sweet visioned face smiled so bright

And I knew that once mounted this diamond
Would for your hands alone be just right
Thus was it that out here while walking
With naught else but you on my mind
I found what your beauty would compliment
When tomorrow you I ask to be mine
With a heart and a love everlasting
Long past when this diamond is dust
Faithful ever to you never changing
In valor, devotion and trust
So say you'll be mine love forever
Make come true the dreams that I hold
Take this diamond as my pledge forever
Surrounded by the finest of gold

May 16, 1977

The answer to
The Foghorn (page 33)
is 71.

Other Collections by This Author:

A Poet's Ebb And Flow

In The Middle of Believe There's A Lie

Inside A Heart

Judge Me Not Without A Trial

Legends, Lives & Loves Along the Inside Passage

Love... Life's Illusive Zenith

Love's Reflections

Love's Refuge and Sonnets

Only Children Of The Universe Are We

Step Scenes Of Life

That We Too Free May Live

~ ~

For more information go to:

www.dncsite.ca

~ ~

www.ingramcontent.com/pod-product-compliance
Lightning Source LLC
Chambersburg PA
CBHW021344090426
42742CB00008B/733